The C

Ayiamagen

Take
a brand new luxury car, and
blaze a trail of unsolved crimes
across four countries !
The following true stories have
been written as accurately as
possible, without exaggeration.
The imaginary portion has evolved
since its original inception, nearly
forty years ago.
Originally printed in an
abbreviated form on
Jan. 11th , 2011
This new version is the
full, uncensored, unedited edition.

James L. Parker
March 13th , 2014
May Your Load
Be Light

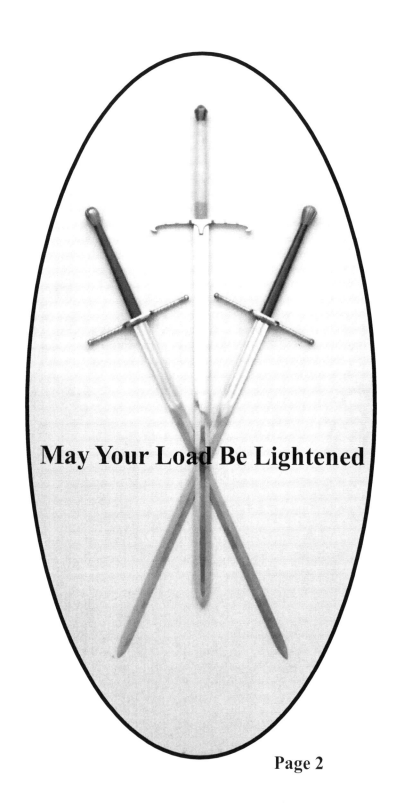

May Your Load Be Lightened

Contents

Earth Entry Station # 2000

Enterdimensional Credit Card and **Imprinted waiver form** Required for entrance into Human form

Staying beyond one's paid excursion, will incur additional fees.

Enter At Your Own Risk !

Jim, 1949

Page 4

Chapter One
Imagination
Station

The pile of old magazines and books in his Grandmothers cellar, reeked of old mold and dust. The smell clogged his airways and stung his eyes, but somehow he knew that there was something in that pile he needed to find.

There was one issue of **'Rosicrucian Digest'**, in poor condition, that caught his eye. Jim carefully separated the fragile pages and looked at each one, until he came to an article titled;

'Thoughts Have Wings'

The article said that thought generates a mental energy which can be projected from ones mind to the consciousness of another, and suggested the following as proof;

Concentrate intently upon another who is seated in a room with you, without his noticing it. Observe that person gradually become restless and finally turn and look in your direction.

Jim practiced while sitting in class. If the receiver was a girl, he might imagine a feather tickling the back of her neck. If it was a boy, a flicking of the ear by a ghost hand was in order.

Besides the tickling and ear flicking, students were often subjected to spit wads, rubber band attacks and other jokes. One of Jim's favorites was the placing of several small lumps of calcium carbide under the seat of another student seated in front of him. The lumps were then wetted with water or spittle, causing an immediate bubbling reaction as the foul smelling gas was released. In a short time the whole class would be looking around to see who had the flatulence problem.

Another favorite often used during lunch break, was the 'sucker shove'. One student would distract the 'sucker' while another student would crouch down on hands and knees, close behind him. The distracter would then shove the sucker over the crouched student, while yelling **'sucker shove'.**

During summer vacation from school, a travelling carnival had come to the small town in the foot hills of southern California, where Jim had grown up.

The carnival had the usual rides and games, including a shooting gallery that gave as one of the prizes, an arrow that bent around one's head, to make it look as though they had been attacked by 'wild Indians'. The sight of people walking around with arrows through their heads gave Jim an idea. What if peoples view of him could be made to follow a path like the arrow around the heads of the carnival goers, wouldn't that make him invisible ?

This bending of sight idea, soon evolved into what Jim called 'Shields'. While walking between classrooms he would imagine a tubular shaped mirror that was reflective on the outside and transparent from the inside. When needed, the 'Shield' would drop over him. The transparent inside allowing a view out, while the mirrored outside shielded him from view. He practiced using 'Shields' frequently, and often imagined the shield around him most of the time, only turning it off occasionally.

Jim didn't think much about it, the first time it happened, but the second time he sat down in a restaurant without being waited on, he began to imagine the possibilities.

On some days, Jim would ride a motorcycle to school. As an 'Auto Shop' project he rebuilt and customized an old English made, **'BSA' 650 cc.**

The final assembly was done at home, in the garage. The new metal flake blue paint looked good, and the engine was ready for a test start. All that was missing were the license plates and lights.

Jim straddled the bike, switched on the ignition, turned on the fuel valve, and turned the engine over using the 'kick starter'. After a few good kicks, the engine roared to life.

It was evening and nearly dark outside, but a quick ride shouldn't be a problem. It was around five miles from the garage to the center of town.

The new exhaust system was louder than expected and would need to have baffles installed. The roar seemed to be attracting a lot of attention from onlookers, including a local police officer in a patrol car. By the time Jim turned around and got back to his home, there were three police cars in pursuit, with lights flashing and sirens wailing. Quickly, Jim turned into the gravel driveway, pulled into the garage, and slammed the door closed. Exiting the garage from a side door, Jim entered the house from the rear door. Jim's Father was inside watching the three patrol cars skid into the driveway, kicking up a cloud of dust. Jim's Father had noticed him leaving on the loud motorcycle, and was waiting at the front window for his return. As Jim interred the house from the rear, his Father, enraged by the cloud of dust and invading police, was already on his way out the front door to greet them. After some very unfriendly vocal exchanges, the police got back into their cars and left. All Jim's father had to say as he reinterred the house was; 'you'd better get some lights on that damned thing'.

Besides high school, Jim spent week ends getting military training as a 'Junior Marine / Devil Pup'. The organization had a camp and training grounds nearby, and also included trips to Camp Pendleton Marine Corps base, where they received hand to hand combat, and weapons training.   Page 8

Jim's Father had been a soldier during World War Two. Though he was left handed, he was forced to learn to shoot right handed, and went on to earn a 'Sharpshooter' metal, shooting right handed.

Jim was taught by his Father, to shoot and tie his shoes left handed, though he was born right handed. As a result, Jim could fire a handgun equally well with either hand, as well as rifles, although the rifle would come up naturally to the left handed position.

A few years after Jim graduated from high school, he knew that it would only be a matter of time before his number came up and he would be drafted into the military for use in the Viet Nam war.

In preparation for the inevitable, Jim decided to prepare with an upgraded 'Shields' program.

The new program would include; Auto activation, reduced pain and fear of death, subconscious choreography, including; distraction, manipulation, confusion, of others, as needed, to achieve an objective. He thought that 'Shields' might work like this;

Suppose that you are in a building and need to get out without being seen. All exits are being watched by men with wireless phones. You use your phone to call one of the watchers, and tell him something that will cause a distraction allowing you a moment to escape.

Now imagine the same scene, but this time without your phone.

This time your subconscious mind wirelessly connects up to one of the watchers and distracts him long enough for you to get away. No magic, just wireless communication.

Installation of the new 'Shields' program, into Jim's subconscious mind was achieved through deep relaxation. After a thorough workout to relax the body, he would lay on his back. The details and intentions for the programs use, already memorized and represented by a symbol. Holding the symbol in his mind, he would tense and release each muscle, starting with the feet and ending at the head. He would repeat the tensing and releasing until his body was tired and relaxed. At this point Jim would imagine stepping into an elevator and pressing the button marked 'Control Room'.

As the elevator ascended, Jim would loose awareness of his body, and scenes would appear. Sometimes fog would clear to reveal a city in the distance, or often it would be a busy outdoor market place. He named this place 'Imagination Station'. As a child, Jim had often seen similar scenes at the foot of his bed, late at night, but never quite in focus. But the images here were crystal clear, and included sound.

Once the elevator reached the control room, and the door opened, Jim would deliver the program in the form of the symbol that represented his intentions for the programs use. The installation was repeated often, and was a good means of getting to sleep.

The town seemed to gradually become an empty and lonely place, as classmates went off to college, or the military. One evening as Jim sat in his car listening to music at a popular teen hang out, four teens from another town pulled into the parking lot and parked their 1964 Chevelle, next to Jim's car. The boys offered to sell Jim the Chevy 'real cheap' as there were no papers. Not wanting the car, Jim turned down their offer. Later the teens admitted to stealing the car, and said they would just leave it there, in the parking lot, for anyone who wanted to take it. After the four boys were gone, Jim decided to take a look at the now abandoned car. He was surprised to find the keys still in the ignition switch.

Jim knew someone that might want to dismantle the car for it's parts. After a brief phone call, Jim picked the man up so he could drive the 'hot' Chevy to his garage, which was equipped with a chain hoist for removing engines. After the car was disassembled, all that was left was the bare body, which was loaded onto a trailer. After a thorough wipe down to remove finger prints, the body was taken to a remote area and dumped from the trailer to slide down into a deep ravine.

After returning to the garage, it was noticed that a jack stand that was used to help keep the body on the trailer was missing. The acquaintance and his helper panicked, thinking that the missing jack stand might have finger prints on it.

It was late night when Jim headed home, telling the two not to worry about the missing jack stand, but they decided to return to the dump site to retrieve it, on their own, only to find the police already there investigating. After being stopped and searched by the police, the two were arrested for the dumping, based on car parts found in their auto. The parts weren't from the dumped car, but were from some previous 'job'. During the police 'questioning' one of the two, implicated Jim, who was arrested later. The 'acquaintance' would later become the subject of a TV program, **Cold Case Files episode #83 'cat and mouse'**. The six month sentence Jim was given, could be shortened by two months if he were to work on a road maintenance crew, made up of prisoners.

While working on the road crew, Jim's military draft number was chosen, and he received a notice to go get a physical examination to determine fitness to serve. After notifying the draft board of his current situation, he received a '4F' card in the mail, making him ineligible for military service. After his release, Jim decided to play a little joke on the local police dept.

FOR SALE
Hot Rod !
1934 Ford 3 window coupe
327 Chevy Engine, Only $150.oo
[police station phone # here]

In Yucaipa, the town that Jim grew up in, there was a publication that took classified advertisements over the phone. You would only be charged if the item sold, and they kept track of people by the phone number posted with the advertisement.

The price of $150. would have been a real bargain, and generated a lot of calls. The officer that answered the phone when Jim called about the 'Hot Rod' didn't seem pleased.

Jim's family had moved to The Dalles, Oregon, a town that sits along the Columbia River. Yucaipa had grown stale, so he decided to join them there.

It was summer of 1970, and Jim had gotten a job at one of the cherry processing facilities in The Dalles. Freshly harvested cherries were put into huge wooden vats, and covered with a brine solution to preserve them. Throughout the year, the preserved fruit would be pumped onto conveyer belts to be sorted out by workers along both sides of the moving belt. One day Jim wondered what would happen if marbles were to suddenly appear on the belt, along with the cherries. He had a jar full at home, and put them into his lunch box the next morning. He had never seen those women move as fast as when those marbles hit the belt.

During lunch break, Jim would sit in his car to eat and listen to music. Another employee named Clay that Jim had become acquainted with, would join him for lunch.

Jim's family lived in a house overlooking the river. The house had a basement bedroom with a private entrance in the rear. One evening Clay stopped by for a visit. During the visit, Jim showed him a collection of old coins that included one gold coin.

After the visit was over, Clay left in his 1950 Plymouth coupe, and Jim got into his Black 1964 Plymouth Fury, and left as well.   Page 13

Later, after returning home, a neighbor called to inform Jim that the man who was visiting him had returned, and was seen entering the house from the rear sliding door. The glass sliding door had a separate screen door in front of it. The screen had been cut allowing it to be unlatched. The glass door was probably secretly unlatched during the visit. The only thing found to be missing, was the one gold coin from the collection.

1964 Plymouth Fury, with 318 V8 engine and three speed automatic transmission.

Jim threaded his belt though a small leather holster, and inserted the Smith and Wesson .38 caliber snub nosed revolver.

After speeding to Clays house on the other end of town, Jim could see that the old Plymouth was not there. Clay lived at his families house, and had an upstairs bedroom. A young boy answered a knock at the front door, and seemed to be the only one there. Jim explained to the boy, that his older brother Clay had taken something from him, and he was going upstairs to look for it in his bedroom.

After searching the bedroom, Jim left without the coin, As he was getting into his car, he could see Clays little brother at the front window, with a phone in his hand.

Clay had a girlfriend, and Jim found his car parked in front of her house. As Jim pulled up to the curb on the opposite side of the street and got out, he could see that there were no lights on in the girlfriends house, and the window shades had been closed. Jim called out several times and honked the car horn, but there was no response.

The fuel gauge on the Fury had quit working, so Jim carried an extra can of gasoline in the trunk in case he were to run out. He poured the fuel throughout the interior of Clay's car. Then splashed the roof and hood, and finally some on each tire.

After getting back into the Fury, Jim backed up so he could pull up close to Clays Plymouth. As Jim slowly passed by, he struck one match, and used it to ignite the entire match book. As he tossed the flaming match book into the open window, Jim hit the accelerator pedal, trying to get clear, but the blast came so quickly that it rocked the Fury and singed his hair and eyebrows. A girl that Jim had been dating lived nearby. The lights were still on at her home when he drove by, so he turned the car around and stopped in front of the house. Linda saw the Fury pull up, and came outside. Jim quickly explained what had just happened, and the two then drove to a parking lot, that overlooked the burning car scene below.

The Dalles Chronicle ran a front page article and photo of Clay looking at the burned out hulk. The article titled 'Mysterious Fire Destroys Automobile' appeared in the Tuesday, September 29, 1970 issue. It said that police and firemen arrived at around 1:10 a.m. and found the car engulfed in flames. People in the neighborhood reported a loud noise, and a series of noises that Clay told police were from exploding handgun ammunition that was inside the car.

The caption under the photograph said that the owner of the car couldn't figure out what happened to his car during the night, and neither could firemen who were continuing the investigation.

The following day, while at his job at the cherry processing facility, Jim, who was now armed with only a .38 caliber, two barrel derringer, saw an angry man walking quickly towards him. He recognized the man as the owner of several local businesses. As the man got near, he placed his hand into his coat, as though ready to draw a weapon, and shouted 'where is that son of a bitch Clay'?, adding that he knew the two of them hung around together. Jim replied; 'you are too late, I torched his car in retaliation for burglarizing my families house, while they were at home upstairs, and I've heard that he left town. The man relaxed, and said that he was relieved, as he really didn't want to shoot anyone. The man explained that his shop had been broken into, along with a restaurant, and some private residences. He blamed the burglaries on Clay.

After the encounter with the angry businessman, there seemed little use in trying to hide the story. Linda surely would have told her family, and others. But Jim was never even questioned by the police about the fire, and never saw Clay again.

On Monday, February 15, 1971, **The Dalles Chronicle** ran an article on the front page that said Clay had been arrested in Albany, Oregon in January, returned to The Dalles, where he was charged with arson, and later, for burglary and grand larceny. Although not convicted for the arson, he received three years in prison for the other charges. Jim assumed that the arson charge that Clay was originally arrested for, was for burning his own car, although the first newspaper article said that the car was not insured. Jim never found out for sure.

After moving into a small house on the outskirts of town, Jim wanted a motorcycle to customize. He headed east, along the Columbia River, to Pasco Washington, where there was a Motorcycle Dealer. They had in stock a full dress 1959 Harley Davidson 1200. Not wanting all those extra accessories, a deal was made to lower the price in exchange for the dealer stripping them off and selling the bike as is. After getting the new project home, in the back of a van, He placed a ramp over the steps leading to the front door, and put it into the house for safe keeping. There was no garage, so the kitchen became the permanent night time parking place for the bike.

1959 Harley Davidson 1200

The new bike was named **Cyclops** because of the large headlight mounted up high.

Jim had a pet parrot named Peabody, that would sit inside an open cage, that was on top of the refrigerator. One day while at a new job, working in a mobile home factory, Jim was leaning against one of the homes that he had just finished a final electrical and plumbing inspection on. He was well ahead on his duties and could afford to relax for a few minutes. He smoked marijuana occasionally, but hadn't had any lately, and never drank alcohol. As he relaxed against the mobile home, a line appeared in front of his face and then expanded to form what looked like a television screen. On the screen, a scene played out in which Peabody was frightened by a loud noise and flew out the front door. The screen then formed back into a line and disappeared.

One afternoon as Jim arrived home from his job, he opened the front door and left it open for some fresh air. He also opened the rear door, which suddenly slammed closed from a sudden gust of wind, making a loud noise, which frightened Peabody, who flew out the front door, never to be seen again.

Peabody posing on Cyclops

One day, after the loss of Peabody, an acquaintance stopped by to say that he had found a ravens nest on the side of a cliff. The nest had two fully feathered chicks that were ready to leave the nest for the first time. After putting together several long pieces of pipe, they were able to reach up to the nest, tipping it so that the birds fell out. The two ravens flapped their wings and tried to fly, but were caught before they could hit the ground. The two birds were not afraid, and soon became very tame and playful. A piece of food thrown into the sky would be caught before hitting the ground. Jim kept one bird and the acquaintance took the other.

After complaints from neighbors about the mischievous raven eating out of their gardens, Jim, concerned that someone might shoot the bird, released it into a safer area.

One hot summer afternoon, Jim had laid down on a waterbed to do a 'Shields booster'. It was too hot for a work out, so he started with the tensing and releasing of muscles, in order to achieve the necessary deep relaxation. As he held the symbol that represented the Shields program in his mind, while continuing the tensing and releasing, Jim lost awareness of his body. Normally, at this point, he would imagine an elevator, but this time his mind began to wonder. He thought about how nice it would be to just float in the clouds. Suddenly, Jim was looking down on a river, with people in white robes, along it's banks. The breeze, from the wings of a flickering white bird, sweeping across Jim's face, caused him to wonder were the breeze had actually came from. He was alone in the house, but the slight breeze felt as though someone had just walked by. He struggled to return to his body, but felt paralyzed. Finally, he was able feel his body again, and sat up to find that he was still alone in the house.

Uniroyal Gold

One of Jim's coworkers at the cherry processing facility, had taken a vacation to Mexico.

While in Acapulco, he purchased a kilo of marijuana. After placing the weed inside of the spare tire, and refilling the tire with air, he mounted the tire on his car, and drove all the way back to The Dalles, Oregon, with the weed spinning around inside of the tire.

The kilo of marijuana had all turned into a fine powder, with a robust flavor, and slight rubber aftertaste.

The Dalles had been interesting, but it was time for some real adventure. After selling off nearly all possessions, including Cyclops, Jim had enough money to take a trip that would test his 'Shields' program for real. Everything he owned could be put into a large suitcase, which he carried with him on the bus journey from Portland Oregon, to San Bernardino California.

It was summer 1975, when Jim had an acquaintance drop him off on one of San Bernardino's popular cruising streets for teens and hot rodders. This wasn't his plan, to be dropped off. Jim had wanted to cruise the city, in order to find an expensive imported automobile, but the driver 'Slick' suddenly became so nervous that he could barely speak. Jim could tell that he would not hold up under any strain, and told the shaken driver to pull over. Jim got out and said; go home, I can find one right here on 'E' street, see you in a few months. Slick and Jim were planning to become partners in a retail store. Jim was raising money for the purchase of the store. Slick worked in a retail store, where he would place coupons cut from newspapers, into the till, and remove the value of the coupons in cash. Jim would push cartloads of merchandise through Slicks check stand, and only get charged a small amount. Slick and Jim would later, divide up the loot. Jim also occasionally worked for Slick's father, painting his rental houses with shiny white paint that was supposed to be used for the white center line on roadways. [As of 2014, 'Slick' remains in office as an elected official in the state of California].

There were many auto dealerships on 'E' street, and just across the street from where Jim had been dropped off was a lot full of new Cadillac automobiles.

After scanning the area, Jim crossed the street to take a look. He didn't like big overweight cars, and these things looked like limousines. The lot was well secured, with each cars exit path blocked, except for one. The green four door, Cadillac Sedan Deville facing 'E' street was blocked only by the sidewalk and curb.

Looking into the window of the small office where salesmen hang out during business hours, he could clearly see a peg board holding the keys for the cars on that lot.

Returning to the sidewalk, Jim noticed a man that he hadn't seen for several years, looking back at him from across the street. Paul ! Jim said as he crossed over to greet his uncle. Paul, I'm in a hurry and I need you to do something for me, Jim said in a low voice. I know what you're up to, Paul replied. While serving that sentence for the stolen Chevy, Jim was waiting in a large holding cell full of prisoners one morning, waiting to be transferred out to the next road maintenance job. Two inmates were kneeing at the feet of a man who was laying on the concrete floor sleeping. One of the men had just ignited a small bundle of matches that had been placed between Paul's toes. Jim had not expected to see Paul, and didn't even know that he was in jail.

Quickly, Jim removed the burning matches and said; 'That's my Uncle !' The one who had lit the matches replied; 'We don't want to screw with your kin' as the two backed away. Paul slept through the whole incident and Jim never mentioned it to him. After Paul's shorter sentence was over, Jim never saw him again until now.

Returning to the car lot office, no alarm system in sight, Jim pulled the small steel pry bar from his coat. The door came open easily. Hanging on a hook next to the keys, were license plates that were used for test drives when trying to sell the cars. The plates were secured by an attached strap that was held in place by having the trunk lid closed over it.

While driving over the curb, Jim waved to Paul, as he headed for the nearest gas station and highway onramp. Paul did not have to whistle, if the security patrol on motorbikes showed up suddenly.

Noticing the dealer plates, the gasoline station attendant quipped; 'Delivering cars eh' ? Dealer swap Jim replied. Palm Springs dealership needs a green one. Don't know what they're sending back. Can't imagine anyone wanting this ugly ass green.

A few days before, Jim had hand written a bill of sale, transferring ownership of some miscellaneous farm equipment from himself to another person. He wrote out the bill of sale on two thin pieces of paper that were glued together at the edges, to make it appear to be only one sheet. He took the document to a 'Notary Public' to have it notarized, making it more official. After showing I.D., Jim signed the document and a gold foil star was affixed.

Next, the foil star that was now stuck firmly on the paper was embossed with an official seal.

Later, after cutting away the edges, the top and bottom sheets were separated. The blank bottom sheet, although without a gold star, still showed an impressive raised seal.

After parking the Cad in an upscale neighborhood where it would blend in, Jim began searching parking lots for another similar Cadillac. It didn't take long to find one, and remove the registration paper from it's holder. The document listed a different color, but that was easily corrected with eraser and typewriter. The license plate numbers were also corrected to match a set of plates taken from a car that wasn't in running condition, and wouldn't be missed right away.

It was impractical to attempt changing the long vehicle I.D. numbers on the new registration to match those on the stolen car, so they were left unchanged. On the blank sheet of paper with the notary seal, Jim wrote out a bill of sale transferring ownership of the Cadillac listed on the registration, to himself. He now had an official looking bill of sale and matching registration document.

The Hydrant Wrench

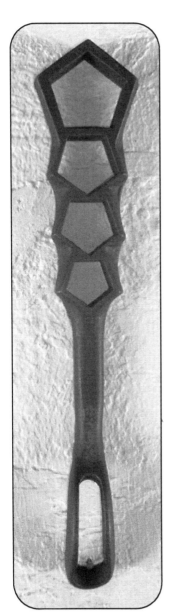

When Jim was around sixteen years old, a truck stopped at the fire hydrant In front of his families house, to fill a large water tank. After the truck left, the wrench was still on the hydrant.

That wrench started a Halloween tradition. Every Halloween, Jim would round up a car load of classmates, and they would race around town turning on fire hydrants.

Aylamagen

Chapter two

Driving through the warm desert air was relaxing, no need for the air conditioning. But, Jim was having trouble keeping his eyes open. I'll pull over along the highway for a few minutes rest, he thought.

As he relaxed into the plush seat, a scene began to appear, foggy at first, then clearing to reveal a roadway. With steep drop offs on either side, and jagged rocks below, one had little choice but to follow the road. Constructed entirely from stone and as wide as a two lane highway, it seemed to disappear at the foot of a great mountain, in the far distance.

Travelers lined the roadway, with the majority heading toward the mountain. Most were on foot, some pushed or pulled carts, loaded with water jugs. Two boys struggling with an overloaded cart caught his attention. Moving in closer, he could hear them arguing about whether or not to jettison part of the load to make it easier to pull.

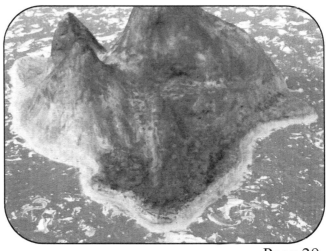

And just imagine, one of the boys was saying, with the money we get from selling this water, we can stay for the entire festival. We can eat, sleep in a real bed, and even treat some of the others. So pull you little sniveler, pull like TRAGAS is on your trail. As the two slowly ascended, the lettering on their black hooded shirts came into view. 'Starats' was all it said.

Up ahead, a guide was explaining to a group of tourists, how the roadway had been constructed long ago. An admission toll of one head sized stone or one standard jug of water was required to use the road, with the stones being used to continue construction toward a plateau on the side of the largest mountain. A treasure trove of water was said to have been discovered there, and with water in such short supply, construction on the roadway continued at a fast pace. Once the roadway reached the plateau, huge rock walls were built on either side of the narrow entrance, with stockpiles of round stones, ready to greet invaders.

Along the roadside, near the entrance to Aylamagen, vendors sold food, water, and souvenirs. Continuing through the gates, the roadway was lined with shops, restaurants, and lodges with spectacular views.

A commotion, at the entrance to a large building was attracting a crowd of onlookers. The building was at full capacity, but more people wanted in. I'm sorry, the doorman was saying, If Maloney shows up, he will jerk our license for sure.

Inside on a small stage, a band was preparing to perform. The drums had strange tattoo like designs, on the skin covered heads. Jim had seen similar symbols being sold at tourist stands near the city gates.

The crowd had become impatient, and had begun to chant; Clancy, Clancy! Clancy!! Finally the announcer appeared, to introduce the next performance. Here they are! The winners of last years shoot out, **Clancy Derringer and The Sky Finger Band !**

OK, OK, calm down now before you blow your corks. I'm Clancy Derringer, and I hope to see you again, at the **ICE Festival**, for the band 'shoot out'. In the mean time, we would like to try something new on you, called; 'Khat Man Dew'

Khat Man Dew

Khat Man Dew Khat Man Dew
Going to see the Khat Man
In Khat Man Dew
All I wanna do
Is go to see the Khat Man
In Khat Man Dew

Told the taxi driver
Take me to
Khat Man Dew
Khat Man Dew Khat Man Dew

Taxi driver said
No can do
Khat Man Dew
Khat Man Dew Khat Man Dew

But I gotta see
The Khat Man
In Khat Man Dew
Khat Man Dew Khat Man Dew

Taxi driver said
But no can do
Khat Man Dew
Can't get through
To Khat Man Dew
Khat Man Dew Khat Man Dew

But man that won't do
I gotta see The Khat Man
In Khat Man Dew
You just gotta get through
To Khat man Dew
Khat Man Dew Khat Man Dew

What's he gunna do ?
Can't get through
To Khat Man Dew
Khat Man Dew Khat Man Dew
Can't get through
To Khat Man Dew Khat Man Dew

 All of a sudden, the drummer took off a
shoe and began pounding on his drum
with it. The band stop playing, and the
room went silent .

You Can't Sleep Here !

Suddenly, Jim realized that someone was banging on the roof of the new Cadillac. He opened his eyes to find a policeman tapping the car with a metal flashlight.

You Can't Sleep Here !
Indio is just up ahead. You can get some coffee or a room for the night there, he said.

I was having trouble staying awake and thought it would be safest to pull over for a few minutes to rest. But that coffee sounds good, Jim replied.
As he started the engine and carefully pulled back onto the highway, it occurred to him that the encounter with the cop was very unusual. The officer didn't ask for his license and registration, which was standard procedure, although, in his experiences, police always called in the license numbers and description of vehicles before getting out of their car.

Jim reasoned, that at some point, the police station might figure out, that those license plates were on the wrong car, and the cop who had awakened him might be coming up fast on his tail even now.

Using imagination, Jim extended a shield wall of invisibility around the moving car, as he watched the speedometer climb.

Legend, In His Own Mind

He's got the Cad.
And heading east
Just a jump ahead
Of the state police
The Car Thief Priest The Car Thief Priest

Decide what to do
And make it fast
Choose wrong
It will be your last
The Car Thief Priest The Car Thief Priest

Ditch the car
And head back home ?
There's nowhere to go
You're all alone
The Car Thief Priest The Car Thief Priest

End of story
Or blaze of glory
The Car Thief Priest The Car Thief Priest

You'll have the whole place talkin
There'll be guns a cockin
If you don't stop movin
Like an old man walkin
The Car Thief Priest The Car Thief Priest

Shields are workin
He's got no fear
Cops are comin
Let's get it in gear
The Car Thief Priest The Car Thief Priest

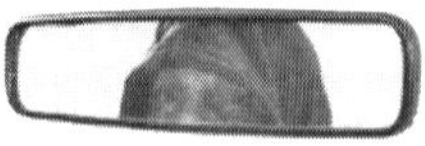

Checkin the mirror
For red lights flashin
Coast is clear
So keep on passin
The Car Thief Priest The Car Thief Priest
Better make way for The Car Thief Priest

Passin through
Without being seen
Playing it cool
In the Green Machine
The Car Thief Priest The Car Thief Priest
Better make way
For The Car Thief Priest

Border comin up fast
Better slow er down
To avoid a crash
The Car Thief Priest The Car Thief Priest
Better make way
For The Car Thief Priest
Everybody's talkin bout

The Car Thief Priest

The Car Thief Priest

The Car Thief Priest

The Car Thief Priest

The Car Thief Priest

The Car Thief Priest

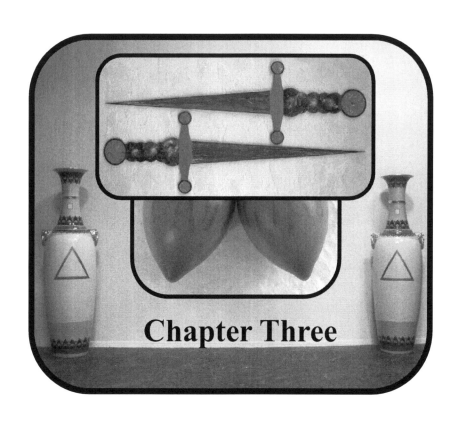

Chapter Three

Big
Twin
Beauties

After making it to the Mexican border, and entering the country with the phony documents, Jim stopped in a familiar neighborhood to make a purchase.

He'd been here before, to purchase a kilo of marijuana. A street vendor who appeared at the car window, said he could get it, but wanted the money up front. No way, you bring it here and I'll pay after I see it, Jim replied. The man agreed and said he would return in fifteen minutes.

Awhile later, the vendor suddenly reappeared at the window with a package crudely wrapped in plastic sheeting, and taped closed. He kept looking back and forth as though he were afraid of being seen, and quickly tossed the package onto the floor of the car, behind the drivers seat, where it would be out of reach. As Jim reached behind his seat to retrieve the package, the vendor, whose face was at the open window, angrily demanded;

Give Me The Money **Now** !

Want to die ? Jim asked, as his right hand pulled and cocked the Ruger .22 caliber single action that was hidden in the center console.

The vendor recoiled at the sight of the revolver, and disappeared into the crowded street, after muttering some choice Spanish insults. The package yielded only some old newspapers.

But this time he wasn't after weed. Spotting a street vendor, an older man, carrying an assortment of tourist items, Jim called out to him; Hey Chief ! as he signaled the vender to come to the car window.

After listening to what Jim was after, the old man unrolled a small cloth bundle, to display the contents. No, no, no, I don't want this cheap tourist crap ! Mass grandee, mass fuerte ! Jim explained as he made a measurement by spreading his hands. Si, si senior, you wait, por favor, the old man asked. Dos, dos !, Jim reminded, as 'Chief' disappeared down a busy street without asking for money first.

As Jim waited for the street vendor to return, a small crowd of onlookers began forming around the new luxury car. Even in a border town, the Cadillac attracted attention.

A short time later, 'Chief' returned with another cloth bundle, larger than the first. As the old man unrolled the bundle to reveal the contents, Jim exclaimed; yes ! That's more like it ! As he picked up one of the twin set of white bone handled knives.

Pressing a button located on one side of the folded knife, released a powerful spring, propelling a flashing steel blade into the open position with such force, that it nearly jumped out of his hand. After pushing the button again, allowing the blade to be refolded, Jim picked up the other matching 'switchblade'. One in each hand, he pressed both buttons at the same time. As the twin blades snapped open, he thought; how intimidating, intimidating twin beauties.

After refueling the car and himself, Jim headed south, into Mexico. He planned to head for Oaxaca, without stopping any more than necessary. **While driving, his mind wandered.**

Gravelsnatch !

When you're at the beach
Better keep it out of reach
Of Gravelsnatch
Gravelsnatch

In the dirt
Might get you hurt
If there's Gravelsnatch
Gravelsnatch

If you're on the floor
Better think some more
About Gravelsnatch
Gravelsnatch

On the grass
Might stain your ass
But there's no need to pass
As there's no Gravelsnatch
Gravelsnatch

In the hay
You'll want to stay
Every day
Cause there's no Gravelsnatch
Gravelsnatch

In the car
You'll go far
Have a treat
In the street
In the moss
Upset your boss
In the air
At the fair
You'll have no care
Anywhere
There's no Gravelsnatch
Gravelsnatch

If you want for more
Better lock the door

If there's Gravelsnatch

The Tree Tomato
or
Tamarillo
[Solanum betaceum]

After arriving in Oaxaca, Jim found an attorney in the phone book, who specialized in automobile sales transactions. After showing the attorney the Cadillac, Jim found out that a luxury car like that could only be purchased by some high ranking government or military official, and he suggested taking it to Guatemala, or some other country further south.

Along the way to Guatemala, Jim stopped at a busy rest area, to take a break from the tedious driving. As usual, when he parked the car, a number of people would gather to take a look. But this time it was different. One nervous traveler warned that the police would plant drugs on your car so they could impound it when the drugs were later 'discovered'. See for yourself, every police car has license plates from some other country, he added.

It was starting to get dark, and Jim was sitting on a park bench at the rest area. He had planned to sleep, as usual, in the rear seat of the car. In the low light, he could see three uniformed men walking around the Cadillac. One stopped, kneeled down, and was looking around one of the front tires. It appeared that he was looking for a place to put something. The three men gathered briefly at the front tire, and then walked away together.

As soon as the three uniformed men were out of sight, Jim got into the car, started the 500 cubic inch engine, and with the tires spitting gravel, he got back onto the highway, and didn't stop again until he came to the Guatemalan border.

The Guatemalan entry paper Jim received, listed the car he came into the country with. If he were to attempt to leave the country without the car, import duty would be charged on the automobile. Import duty on a luxury car could be as much as the value of the car, doubling it's cost to anyone without an exemption from the import duty.

1975 Cadillac Sedan de Ville
500 cubic inch, 210 hp V8 engine

White Raven

Chapter four

While cruising around Guatemala city in the big car, Jim started to pass by the National Palace. A uniformed guard must have mistakenly thought that the big green sedan was a government or military limo, as he stepped into the road, stopped the traffic, and then directed Jim to park in a spot next to the palace entrance.

After parking, Jim entered the palace from the front door, and exited at another door, to explore the city on foot. Having the guard stop traffic and direct him to a parking spot became routine, and afforded a safe place for the car.

Not far away, Jim found another parking spot, in a busy area, near restaurants and shops. After putting 'For Sale' signs on the car, he started walking around, while keeping it in view.

'You need a haircut', a female voice said from behind him. My salon is right over here, one of my girls can take care of you. The salon owner had seen the for sale signs on the Cadillac, and was full of questions. Why are you selling it ?, she asked, to which Jim replied with a now standard answer. I don't want to drive all the way back home, I want to fly.

In the next seat, a young European man was having his hair cut, but was keeping the girl so flustered with his flirting, that she was near tears. How do you say; I want to try your lips, in Spanish he asked. Labios means lips, that's all I know, Jim replied. At hearing that, the young lady left, to be replaced by the salon owner, to finish the job.

The young European man, Hob, who seemed to be well off, was interested in the Cadillac for himself, but didn't know anyone with an exemption from the import duty. Hob was anxious to show Jim around the city, and the two became acquainted.

The owner of a textile factory contacted Jim after seeing the for sale signs on the Cadillac. With the factory owner driving, they set out on a test drive. Along the way, a costumed woman, with a basket of produce balanced on her head, stepped from the left, into the clear lane that went in the opposite direction. At the same time, a car that was following behind the Cadillac, began to overtake it, pulling into the lane now occupied by the produce lady. The impact occurred just to the left of the Cadillac, with bits of glass expanding outward as the headlight shattered, Jim could see her face as she slammed into the windshield, and then seemed to shot forward, tumbling over the pavement as the driver hit the brakes.

Farther down the road, it was getting dark, and had started to rain. A man with a limp human body in a wheelbarrow, was in the middle of the road waving frantically. Can't stop, it's a trap ! The driver said as he maneuvered past them, adding; robbers are waiting in the jungle.

The factory owner wanted to purchase the car, but was unable to find anyone with an exemption from the duty, to purchase it for him.

Hob was anxious to show off his car, a 1961 Chevy convertible.

After parking the Cadillac in a secured lot, Hob and one of his friends named Pax, got into the front seat of the convertible, while Jim got in the rear seat behind Pax. With Hob driving, they headed for a 'Dairy Queen' restaurant for some western style food. Jim only wanted ice cream, and ordered the largest size milkshake on the menu.

After finishing their meals, the three got back into Hob's Chevy, planning to cruise around the city streets. As they proceeded down a 'street', Hob floored the gas peddle, quickly accelerating the classic Chevy to high speed. As they neared an intersection, an empty school bus was coming fast from the right, without slowing, as the bus had the right of way, being on an 'avenue'. The bus struck the Chevy in the right side, forming a tee shape. The impact drove the window crank into Jim's right forearm, near the elbow, throwing him to the other side of the car. The two in the front seat, though shaken, didn't have any obvious injuries, and the bus driver was not injured either. Besides the bleeding gash in his arm, Jim had other minor cuts and was seeing 'stars'.

An ambulance came quickly, and took them to a hospital, where a tube was put into their noses to pump their stomach. If any blood were to be found, it could indicate an internal injury.

The fresh strawberry milkshake, being pumped from Jim's stomach, had attracted a small crowd of people who were debating the meaning of the bright red particles.

They all got a good laugh, when Jim told them about the shake.

Hob and Pax were released later the same evening, while Jim was kept overnight. As he lay there in the hospital bed, the overwhelming smell of antiseptic filled his nostrils.

The smell took him back to around 1969. He had just arrived in Eugene Oregon, and rented a small house, near River Road, in the Santa Clara district. The house was in serious need of a good cleaning. After returning from a nearby market, with cleaning supplies, he gave the place a thorough scrubbing, and sprayed with several cans of antiseptic. The sickening fumes from the spray made the house temporarily uninhabitable.

While waiting for the house to air out, Jim drove to a nearby park, where a young woman came over to listen to the music coming from his car stereo. She asked if he could give her a ride home, and said that she had some good 'smoke' waiting there.

At her house, they smoked marijuana and listened to music. It was late evening when she told Jim, he would have to go, before her 'old man' got home.

Here, she said as he was leaving, the best mescaline that I've ever seen. One for you, and one for a friend. I don't have any friends, Jim replied, as he dry swallowed both of the capsules. You had better drive home quickly ! she exclaimed, adding; 'while you still can'.

Although the house still had a strong smell of antiseptic when he returned, there was nowhere else to go. At around 2:00 A.M. the mescaline started to come on, as the room swirled in colorful stained glass patterns.

A good time to go out for a jog, and some fresh air he thought. Jim put on his dark blue navy 'P' coat, to shield against the cold damp air. As he jogged, Jim felt as though he were running in the clouds. As buildings on the ground came into view, he transformed into a glowing white raven. The feeling was exhilarating, as cool, moist air, swept through his feathers.

As he flew in the clouds, Jim noticed that he was also aware of his legs running on the street at the same time.

The police patrol car heading in the opposite direction, skidded to a stop, and reversed direction, after passing Jim running down the residential street. The lone officer wanted him to get into the front passenger seat, while he explained why he was running down the road at 2;00 A.M. As Jim explained about the bad smell from the antiseptic and wanting to get some fresh air, the policeman's face began to change. Hair, teeth, and beards, grew and retracted. The officer became a man with thousands of constantly changing faces.

Before leaving the house, Jim had placed a knife between his pants and belt, in the back, and then put on the thick wool coat.

As Jim was sitting in the patrol car, watching the officers face transforming, the knife hidden at his back was digging into his skin, and prevented him from sitting all the way back into the seat.

The knife was hand made by Jim's Father's Father. Jim's Grandfather had originally made a matching set for his son, who was in the army. As Jim's Grandfathers son was sticking one of the knives into the wooden floor of the barracks, it broke. The blades had been made from files, and may have been brittle.

OK, you can go, but you may want to choose a better time to do your jogging, the officer scolded as he drove away.

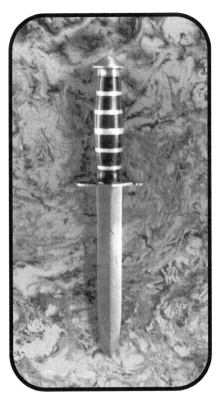

After being released from the hospital, Jim rented a hotel room where he could recuperate for a few days. As he lay there, relaxed, knowing that no one would disturb him, the familiar fog that would clear to reveal another place, appeared.

Welcome to the ' Talked on Larget' show
Here's your host;

Tom Larget

Good evening everyone ! I'm Tom Larget, and you are 'Locked on Target' with Tom Larget
We have plenty to talk about, so let's get right to it.
A tense situation at the north entrance to New California this morning, when TRAGAS agents turned back construction workers who refused to submit to the new URF scan.
Starting today, no one may enter the new 'City of The Future' without the scan.

Testing of the wireless radiant energy system began with a crackle, as a visible corona formed around the doughnut shaped emitters. Lighting tubes, with no wires attached , suddenly lit up, while a myriad of unmanned flying machines, took to the sky. The new city is scheduled to go fully online, in only 30 days from now.

To help us understand this new technology, we've asked our very own 'Professor Peabody' to explain. The Professor is so smart, that when asked if there is anything he doesn't know, he just says; I don't know !

Professor, what's up with these new scanners ?

Thanks Tom

Everything has an energy field that can be detected, Humans have an aura, or energy field, that fluctuates according to the person's emotional state. Though each aura is unique, the fluctuating field made it difficult to pin down, until now. The URF or 'Unique Radiation Field' scanner, can filter out the fluctuating energy, and get a clear shot at the core. The URF scan will replace the old fingerprint I.D. method.

Thanks Professor.

The 'ICE' Festival is in full swing, and we have live coverage for you from Orbicularis Stadium, in Aylamagen, where **Original Blue** is standing by. Original ?

Yes Tom, I can barely hear you, as the crowd has gone wild !

This is the final round, of the band shoot out. The remaining three contestants, do their best, to imitate the ICE One. The metered cheering of the audience, determines the winner, by lighting up the huge stained glass representation of our Mother Planet, Orbicularis.

The winner of last years shoot out, is coming up next. Stand by for; **Clancy Derringer and The Sky Finger Band,** performing;

'My Crackers Are Cracked !'

On each corner of a large triangle, a drummer stands with sticks in hand. In unison, they beat, faster and faster, symbolizing the raising anger of the plaintiffs.

The accused, in the center of the triangle, falls to the floor in pain, as the main curtain opens.

With only a gesture of his hand, a path clears through the angry mob, who have begun to chant

Injure

Cripple !

Exterminate !   Page 56

What's the matter !
Were your crackers cracked ?

If you want an attack
Then show me some facts
Otherwise, get in the back

Ma'am, I don't give a damn
If your cat has been rammed
Smashed by a cycle
Or bottled with jam
Boiled in oil
Or baked with a ham

Just bring me some bad guys
And I'll break out the band
Now I'm not talking a slap on the hand
It's more like cross em
Now wouldn't it be awesome
Wouldn't it be grand
If their blood ran red in the sand

Slap it to em
Stick it to em
Hang em bang em
Reach for the sky
Finger in the eye

Slap it to em
Stick it to em
Poke em choke em
Reach for the eye
Finger in the sky

Slap it to em
Stick it to em
Rope em dope em
Redirect the eye
Finger in the pie

Slap it to em
Stick it to em
Stomp em romp em
Throw em in a sty
Keys in the sky

Slap it to em
Stick it to em
Nail em jail em
Punch em in the eye
Once for every lie

Thank You
May Your Load Be Light

Welcome to the **ICE festival !**
Brought to you by;
Thought Harvester 2000

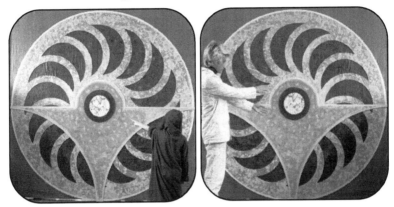

And The Following Fine products and Services

Bottomless Pure Lake Water
Roach For The Sky
Witch At The Steak Sauce
Stripin Chick Chikin Strips
Porkboinksters Restaurants

Roach For The Sky !
Ant and Roach Powder

Fire It Up !
Fire Up Your Meat !
With 'Witch At The Steak' Sauce

Pox E. Doodle's
Strippin Chick
Chikin Strips

Available in 1 and
5 Kilo pre sliced slabs

Introducing The;
Thought Harvester 2000
Information Machine

For a Free Demonstration
Please step up and **Attune Yourself**
The **TH2000**, will update you, on the most current
events.

TH2000 Update;

Along with the population, water harvesting has grown in Aylamagen, to the point that lower areas are seeing a diminishing supply. Lloyd E. Hellslinger 3rd, Commander of TRAGAS Enforcement, has vowed to destroy all unlicensed water harvesting equipment, and arrest the 'water squatters'. Water must be available for New California.

Welcome To

New California

The City of the Future
Here Today
Applications for residency
accepted at any
TRAGAS Enforcement station

URF Scan required for application.

TRAGAS Commander
Lloyd E. Hellslinger 3rd

Inspects the new URF aura tracking missile launcher.
Missiles can locate and lock on to any person who has a URF scan
on file, or may be set to select only hostiles, as determined by their
aura emanations.

The tracker is on your trail
With power from the sky
It's motors will never die
With your aura it will link
It's lethal preservative
Will stop the stink
In your home you may hide
But round and round
For years on end
It will circle your house
And never die

TRAGAS

Enforcement

A family owned business, originally formed to protect the public, from predatory worship organizations. Their duties now include, general law enforcement, and control and distribution of the limited water supply. The meaning of the name 'TRAGAS', has been lost in antiquity.

John Maloney
TRAGAS
Agent

It has been rumored that John Maloney was reproduced from remains taken from the grave of an ancient hunter, who was renowned for his skill at capturing outlaw priests, with a bounty on their heads.

Sean na Sagart's tree

Branches bent and flowers no
Gawkers plenty, he just had to go
That story's over
But there's plenty more
Maloney's back
And lookin to score
Back from beyond
And here to play
Alive and well
This is his day
Carrying a grudge
That someone will pay
Cruising the streets
To earn his way
It's a pity
But he's been set free
They just wouldn't let him be
Neath Sean na Sagart's tree

STARATS
STARATS

We get the water by moon light
If TRAGAS shows up
There will be a fight

Bottomless Lake

Always full, being fed by underground
mountain springs.
The main reason for the building of Old Stone
Highway, and the existence of Aylamagen.
Source of income for the city, when sold
as bottled water.

Bottomless

Pure Lake Water

Bottoms
Up !
with
Bottomless
Pure
Lake
Water

The Order of
Wooden Talisman Wielders

Now considered dogmatic, ritualistic, contrived and limiting. The 'Wielders' were once a powerful worship organization, with far reaching influence, before being hunted to near extinction, by TRAGAS.
The Wielders held strict control over the limited water supply, using their own army of Mantis Warriors to enforce usage restrictions.
The 'Wielders' continue to flourish underground.

ƧMAЯЯAMS

Scientific Method Afterdeath Researchers

May Your Load Be Light, In The Afterdeath

Coming Soon !
RAMS Guide to
Clear Channel Thinking

Aylamagen Eyes

Originally used by bounty hunters and
'Swords for Hire'.
This symbol later came to mean that the
displayer was under the protection of
The ICE One.

Aylamagen Eyes
let potential trespassers know
that they are being watched.

This concludes your free TH2000 update
Now, back to the Festival !

Clancy Derringer

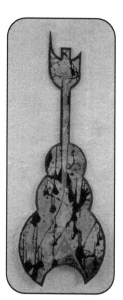

and
The Sky Finger Band
@ The ICE Festival

Senior Boxing !

Puncho Via

Takes on any senior citizen over the age of seventy five.

Proof of age required for entry.

Stand by for Ming
Coming up next

The ICE one Cometh

You've ravaged, plundered
Pillaged and stole
So many times
It's really gotten old

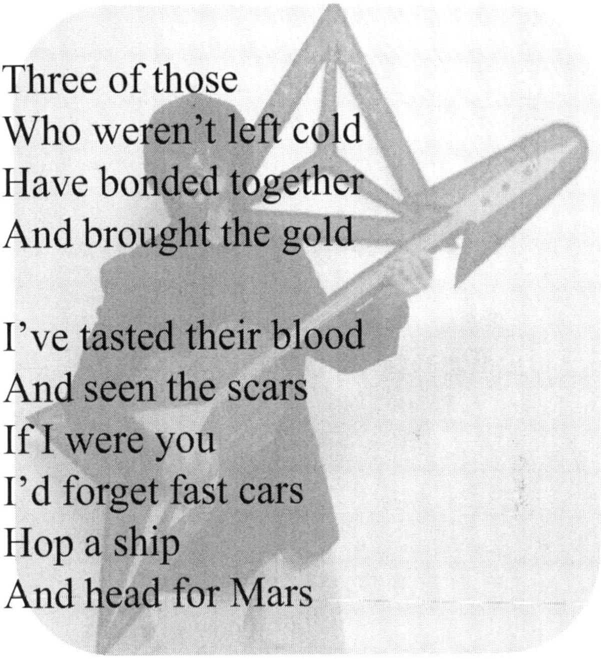

Three of those
Who weren't left cold
Have bonded together
And brought the gold

I've tasted their blood
And seen the scars
If I were you
I'd forget fast cars
Hop a ship
And head for Mars

Don't look for me
I can't be seen
I'm in your mind
To make you scream

You can pull your hair
And pound your head
By nights end
You're gunna be dead

Dead on his feet
Red as a beet
Dry from the heat
Like an old piece of meat

Run fast, don't look behind
Or you'll soon be lost
In the desert of your mind
Scorching winds
Stinging sand
Bleached bones
Across the land

It makes no difference
Woman or man
The ICE One can get you
And you know that he can

Can't run, can't hide
Can't live on the street
They'll snitch you off
For something to eat

Can't think, can't move
Not even begin
It's a sorry state
You've gotten yourself in

It makes no difference
Near or far
The ICE One can get you
Where you are

Your mind is reeling
And you've got no clue
About what the ICE One
Can do to you

Run fast
Don't look behind
All you'll see
Is the twisted train wreckage
Of your mind

Thanks for attending
The Festival
Hope to see you again
Next year

For information about the **ICE Festival**
Call; **Helen Wait**, at the Fairgrounds.

Car Thief Priest

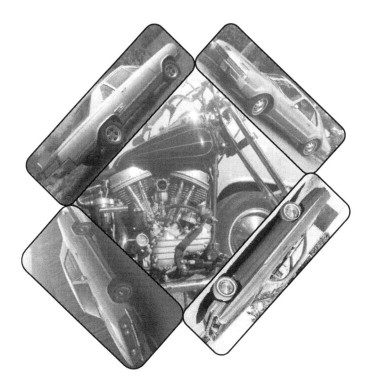

Chapter Five

1964 Buick Riviera

425 cubic inch, 340 horse power V8 engine with three speed automatic transmission.

This luxury car had a hidden windshield wiper switch that was activated with one's foot. Jim would fool passengers by having the wipers magically follow his finger.

1966 Oldsmobile Toranado
425 cubic inch V8 engine
385 horse power
3 speed automatic transmission
Front wheel drive

1961 Pontiac Ventura
389 cubic inch, 267 hp V8 engine.
Three speed automatic transmission.

1965 Oldsmobile 442

4 Four barrel carburetor
4 Four speed, on the floor
2 Duel exhaust pipes

400 cubic inch V8 engine
345 Horse power
4 speed manual transmission

After a few days at the hotel, Jim decided to stay at a campground near Guatemala City.

While at the campground one morning, sitting on a bench, reading a black book with gold lettering on the cover, Jim was approached by a stranger, who had noticed the new Cadillac and book. **What are you,** some kind of **priest or something ?** He asked.

The book, **The Shariyat Ki Sugmad book #2,** was the only reading material Jim had brought with him, and he had already read it several times. One woman who overheard Jim explaining to the stranger, about the subject of the book, became upset, and said; I pray to 'Him' and he provides. I know, but you can get the same results praying to a head of cabbage, Jim replied.

It seemed like a good time to take the Cadillac out for a drive. Along the road, children waited with bags of freshly harvested hallucinogenic mushrooms, which triggered a memory of driving down a country road, late at night, during an ice storm. Jim had gone to a music concert in Medford Oregon. A young man at the concert wanted to trade a 'hit' of LSD, for a ride home after the concert. While 'Eric Burdon' was performing, freezing rain coated the roads with 'black ice' making them extremely slippery.

Besides the crystal faces staring into the windshield, the LSD was causing double vision, which caused the memory of a drunk being asked; how do you manage to drive while seeing double ? I just drive right down the middle, was his reply.

Driving down the middle worked, and Jim was able to deliver the young man, to his home, as agreed.

Tired of trying to sell the car in Guatemala, Jim decided it was time to move on, and headed for the El Salvador border.

Along the way, Jim pulled into a rest area for a break. While he was sitting there, a man approached from a Buick that was parked nearby. The traveler explained that the road ahead, was known for having robbers who would attack lone automobiles. He suggested that the two of them drive together, through the dangerous area, for safety.

After passing through the dangerous area together, the two stopped for a meal. The traveler explained that he was on his way to Costa Rica, where he had a house near the ocean.

The restaurant also had a dormitory, where tired travelers could rent a bed for the night. While sitting in the dormitory, reading The Shariyat Ki Sugmad, the traveler, who had also rented a bed, asked Jim, about the subject of the book. As Jim explained, he could see interest growing on the travelers face. Suddenly the man interrupted, asking; what does it say about homosexuals ? Jim replied that there was no mention of them in the book. May I see the book ? The man asked.

While reading from the first page he opened to, the travelers expression changed. Handing the book back to Jim, and pointing, he said; this lets me out, right here.

The paragraph the traveler was pointing to, clearly stated that homosexuals were not permitted into that organization [Eckankar]. Jim was baffled, he'd read that book several times, and would have remembered seeing it, had it been there.

The traveler retired to his bed, looking depressed, and after a few hours, Jim, unable to sleep, got back into the Cadillac, and went on, alone.

Cowboy With No Hat

Chapter Six

After arriving in San Salvador, the capitol of El Salvador, Jim found a hotel with a fenced and guarded parking lot.

After placing an advertisement for the Cadillac in a local newspaper, he headed back to the hotel. As Jim was nearing his room, three men in cowboy hats were just leaving a nearby room. Where's your hat cowboy ? one of the men called out. I'm the cowboy with no hat, Jim replied.

While he waited at the hotel, for a reply to the advertisement, Jim became acquainted with the three cowboys. After exchanging stories, he learned that the three were from Texas, though living in Belize.

Tired from the journey, Jim relaxed in his hotel room, slipping back into Imagination Station.

Greetings from the **ICE** Festival
Windy and The Footstep Angels
Performing **'No legged Man'**
Are coming up next !

Windy
and the
Footstep Angels
Performing;
No Legged Man

No legged man
Run as fast as you can
The ICE One will get you
And you know that she can
No Legged Man No Legged Man
Run as fast as you can

The boys on the farm
Are gunna sound the alarm
The warnings on your limbs
Are gunna do you harm
No Legged Man No Legged Man
Run as fast as you can

Your fame has spread
Across the land
But the enemies you made
Are now at hand
No Legged man No Legged Man
Better run
As fast as you can

One's a lot
Two's too many
Three's the line
And you've got plenty

You've got some money
And a set of wheels
But hell itself
Is on your hells
No Legged Man No Legged Man
Better run
As fast as you can

One's a lot
Two's too many
Three's the line
And you've got plenty

Rush rush rush !
Hurry hurry hurry !
Your brain's being scrambled
So no more worry
No Legged Man No Legged Man
Better run
As fast as you can

One's a lot
Two's too many
Three's the line
And you've got plenty

Hell, like the desert
Gets bold at night
If the bites don't get you
You'll die of fright
Better run No Legged man
Better run

One's a lot
Two's too many
Three's the line
And you've got plenty

She will torch your mind
And spread the ashes
Or throw them out
With other trashes
No Legged Man No Legged Man
Better run
As fast as you can
Better run
As fast as you can
Better run
As fast as you can

A knocking at the door, brought Jim back to wakefulness. Someone was calling about the Cadillac, and he would have to take the call at the main desk, as there was no phone in his room.

Better Run !

'**No Legged Man**' was first published on Jan. 11, 2011 in the **First Printing** of this book.

A man representing the interested party, wanted to inspect the automobile, and if satisfactory, would arrange for him to see it. Jim had previously hired someone to wash and vacuum the car, and it still looked showroom fresh.

After inspecting the car, and not mentioning the ugly green color, the representative wanted to take it directly to the prospective purchaser. After a short drive, he pulled the car up next to the curb, in front of a large pharmacy. As he leaned over to get out of the car, a Smith & Wesson 44 magnum revolver fell from under his coat, into the gutter. Cursing in Spanish, he retrieved the large hand gun, and returned it to it's holster. Several people came from the pharmacy to quickly view the car.

OK, said the representative, now we are going to an army base, to meet the colonel. It occurred to Jim that he had never though much, about who might purchase the car, but an army Colonel ? This could be dangerous.

After entering the base, the car was stopped at an office building. Several people emerged to view the car, including the Colonel and a woman who would handle the transaction paperwork. Jim explained to the Colonel and the secretary how the car had been signed over to him by a 'notary public', because there was not enough time to go through the normal procedure, as he was leaving soon for a tour through Mexico and Central America. And, now that he had finished the tour, he decided to sell the car and fly home.

During the conversation, it was learned that the Colonel's family was planning a trip to the USA, to purchase a new Cadillac, and they were delighted to find one delivered to their door.

A sale price of $11,000 U.S. dollars, was agreed upon, which was around the cost of the car when new. The payment was to be made in local currency, unless Jim wanted to wait several days for them to exchange the money into U.S. dollars. The documents allowing Jim to leave the country without paying import duty, would take several days as well. Jim decided to accept the local currency, and the secretary began the paperwork. At one point during the paperwork, the secretary called him to the windshield of the Cadillac. Pointing to the vehicle I.D. numbers, visible through the glass, she wanted to know why they didn't match the numbers on the registration. I don't know, Jim replied, but it looks like someone made a mistake. Adding; if I were you, I would use the numbers on the car, rather than the ones on the registration. The secretary agreed, and proceeded with the transaction. After the paperwork was complete, and Jim was paid, in cash, the representative drove him back to the hotel. He was to receive a phone call, when the duty exemption papers were ready.

As he entered the hotel, the three cowboys were at the front desk checking out. Hey guys !, are you heading out ? Jim asked the three, explaining quickly, that he had sold the Cadillac and needed a ride to Guatemala City.   Page 98

Jim told the cowboys that he had put the money from the sale of the car, into a bank, for safekeeping, although it was still in his pockets. We can squeeze you in, if you don't mind riding in a Ford truck, replied the one who would be driving. As they drove toward the border, Jim explained that he wouldn't be able to cross the border with them, as his entry papers showed that he came into the country with an automobile. Jim asked that they drop him off near the border crossing, where he would sneak across on foot.

Patting his front pants pockets, he could feel them there, the Big Twin Beauties, one in each pocket, along with a large wad of cash.

No need, spoke up the driver, we've been through here before. He explained his plan as they neared the border outpost.

As the cowboy's pickup truck was being inspected, the four proceeded to two different office windows, to take care of paperwork. Jim followed along with the cowboys, but tried to stay out of view of the people behind the windows.

Returning to the truck, Jim got in first, rolling himself into a tight ball, on the floor. As the cowboys got in, they placed all of their gear on top of him, and put their legs over him as well.

Don't move a muscle, the driver whispered, as they neared the armed guards, at the exit gates. After a quick look at the exit approvals of the three, the guard waved them through.

As they neared the entry outpost for Guatemala, Jim got out from under the pile of gear.

All Jim needed to do now, was to obtain an entry visa for Guatemala, showing him as being without an automobile. After getting their entry papers, the four headed for Guatemala City, where the cowboys dropped Jim off, and continued on their way to Belize

Hey Cowboy
Where's Your
Hat ?   Page 101

Cowboy with no hat

This may seem strange
But I don't like it
Out on the range

It gets cold at night
And there's things that bite
Eat beans by firelight

Where's your hat cowboy ?

All day chores
And saddle sores
Coyotes howl
No one says good night
Rustlers out lookin for a fight

But I'm a cowboy
A cowboy with no hat
And I kinda like it like that

Where's your hat cowboy ?

I do a little of this
And a little of that
Smoke some of this
And drink some of that

When it's my turn up to bat
I get a little of this
And a little of that

Where's your hat cowgirl ?

But I'm a cowboy
A cowboy with no hat
And I kinda like it like that

I don't horse around
I like my feet on the ground
But I'm a cowboy
A cowboy with no hat
And I kinda like it like that

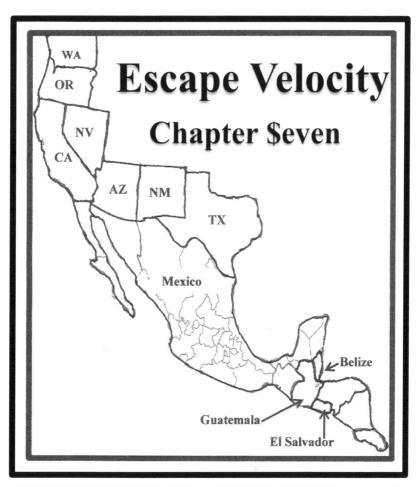

Escape Velocity
Chapter $even

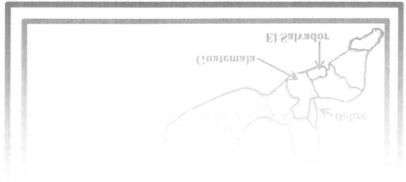

Back in Guatemala City, Jim began exchanging the El Salvador money for U.S. dollars, in small amounts, so as not to arouse any suspicion. Once the money was all exchanged, he went to the airport, to arrange his return flight to California. After the ticket had been purchased, Jim went to admire an old coin display, that had been set up in one area of the airport. As he was looking at a glass display case, containing an assortment of gold coins, he noticed that one of the sliding doors on the back side, that had once been made of glass, had been replaced with a flexible hardboard material, that could be bent outwards, and slid over the top of the lock, allowing access to the contents. Well now, wouldn't this be a good 'Shields' test, Jim though to himself. He couldn't see any cameras or security guards in the area. Thinking to himself again; Do 'Shields' work or not ?, well, let's find out ! At that, he reached over the display case, pulled out on the flexible door, slid it open, and picked up as many coins as he could hold in that one hand. After pocketing the coins, he slid the door closed.

While waiting for his flight, Jim sat down to read, still looking for that lost paragraph, in the Shariyat Ki Sugmad, that was no longer there. As his flight began the boarding process, and Jim got up to get in line, he placed the book on the seat, and left it there.

Now reaching escape velocity, Jim thought to himself, as the plane accelerated down the runway. As a light, relaxed feeling, melted him into the cramped seat, he began to review the incredible adventure. It seemed dreamlike, yet here he sat, with more than $10,000. dollars in cash remaining, along with a pocket of gold coins. Suddenly, the rear of the plane bucked, sending startled passengers, back to their seats, and prompting a turbulence warning from the pilot. The turbulence and frightened passengers, reminded him of the time in Yucaipa, when a fire broke out, in an old, two story, wooden building, near the center of town. Jim was driving a 1966 Plymouth Barracuda through town, with a girlfriend in the front, and her two brothers in the back seat, as the building was burning. The fire trucks were just arriving, and the street hadn't been closed off yet. The street, Yucaipa Boulevard, was lined with people, as if a parade were going by. After passing by the fire, Jim spun the Barracuda around, and headed back, toward the burning building. Just before reaching the fire, he reached for the ignition key, turning it to the off position. As the car, still in gear, and rolling, built up unburned fuel in the exhaust system, Jim reached again for the ignition key, returning it to the on position. As the unburned fuel in the muffler system ignited, the blast, loud as a cannon, sent people scrambling for cover. The four pranksters were then amazed, to see a man running up behind the car, shaking his fist at them. The second blast, sent him back to the sidewalk, as the four laughed hysterically.   Page 106

The Backfiring Barracuda

1966 Plymouth Barracuda
Formula 'S'
273 4v V8 engine
4 speed manual transmission

Escape Velocity

He's got the money
And a pocket of gold
Another story
To be told

The road was long
The ride was soft
500 cubes under the hood
Robin Hood, never had it so good

It's been fun
But it's time to go
On to the next
Before we get old

What lies ahead
A nice warm bed ?
By morrows end
We could all be dead

No need to rewind
Time to unwind
Leave this place behind

Your mind's a balloon
Carry a tune
Away to the moon

Wave goodbye
To the old buffoons
Gathering speed
We'll be there soon

The only remaining coin, from the airport heist.

As he relaxed into his seat, during the flight to California, Jim slipped back into **Imagination Station.**

At a top secret meeting, Hellslinger explains his plan to a hand full of agents.

So, you see, we won't wait for New California's wireless energy transmitter to come on line, as expected. Our research and development lab, has come up with a means to project a directional beam of energy, from behind a huge mobile deflector. This beam of energy will be aimed at Aylamagen, and will power our new aura trackers. Let them roll all the stones they like, our deflector will simply guide them aside. And we will launch this surprise attack, on the final day of their beloved festival. You will occupy the city, and secure Bottomless Lake. Our engineers will begin construction of a temporary pumping station, as soon as the city is secured. You all have your orders, now get moving.

As the agents leave the top secret meeting, to begin preparing for the surprise attack, one of them goes to his office, to move a small potted plant, from his desk, to the window sill.

Some distance away, hidden in the brush, a member of the Starats, closes his looking glass, and slips away, unnoticed.

Original Blue

Later, at a temporary field office, near the entrance to New California, an out of breath young man, excitedly pounds on the door. Original ! Original !, I seen it ! the plant, the signal. Quickly, Original grabs her gear, and follows the young man. These meetings with the TRAGAS agent made her nervous, and she hated the way he looked at her, but he didn't signal for her unless it was something important.

After hearing of the planned surprise attack, from the TRAGAS agent, Original thought to herself; I've got to tell Tom, He will know what to do. If I can get him away from that damned witch, Windy, long enough.

Tom, I'm sorry to interrupt your luncheon with Windy, but this can't wait.

As Original explained to Tom about the planned surprise attack on Aylamagen, they both noticed the nearly deserted streets, which were usually busy, at this time of day. Tom was then distracted by an incoming call, from Professor Peabody, who told him to come to the studio right away, as something big was happening on Old Stone Highway.

ASAP News Flash !
Festival Goers Trapped !
Tom Larget reporting

TRAGAS Enforcement has set up a road block on Old Stone Highway. Festival goers trying to return home, who refuse to submit to a URF scan, are being turned back. We'll keep you informed on this breaking news story, as details become available.

What are we going to do Tom ?
I just have to get through that
Road block. I have to get home,
to Aylamagen.
Don't worry Windy, I know
someone who can get us through.

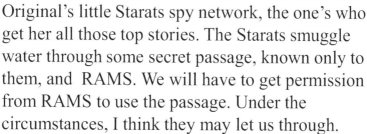

Original's little Starats spy network, the one's who
get her all those top stories. The Starats smuggle
water through some secret passage, known only to
them, and RAMS. We will have to get permission
from RAMS to use the passage. Under the
circumstances, I think they may let us through.
 Two Starats, nick named, 'Nut and Bolt', lead Tom
and Windy through the water smuggling path, that
runs along the base of Old Stone Highway. As they
neared the sheer cliffs that made Aylamagen so
inaccessible, it seemed that there was no where to
go, except straight up.
 Stand back ! Ladder coming down, shouted a voice
from above.
 The ladder lead up to a small opening in the cliff
face. A tall man, in a white uniform, was there to
greet them. The man motioned for Tom, Windy,
Nut and Bolt, to enter a doorway, and then he
closed the heavy metal door. After locking the door
behind them, he turned and said; welcome to
RAMS, please follow me.
 The narrow tunnel, led to a dimly lit room,
furnished with an oval table, some chairs, and a
large RAMS logo, on one wall.

Welcome to RAMS.

 We know of your situation, and have been expecting you. There is no time to waste, as TRAGAS has already begun the attack on Aylamagen. Hellslinger's deflector has begun the assent up Old Stone Highway, and when it reaches the city gates, all hell will break loose. Aylamagen will be overrun quickly. In the past, The ICE One would have shielded us from such an attack, but since she died, without leaving a successor, we are left unorganized and nearly defenseless. But, we must go now, to Aylamagen, to do what we can, to defend the city, and the lake. We shall pass by the tomb of the last ICE One, if you would like to pay your respects.

You boys come along too, as we may have further need of your services.

The RAMS representative lead them through an ever ascending tunnel, until they came to a cavern. A single flickering flame, cast eerie shadows against the walls.

There it is, the tomb of the last ICE One, the RAMS representative said, while pointing to the far end of the room. He went on to explain that the tomb was adorned with a death mask, cast from the face of the ICE One, before placing her body into a preservation chamber.

As they walked toward the tomb, Windy took Tom's hand and said; Tom, there's something I haven't told you.

Just a minute, Windy, Tom said as he looked closely at the death mask.

Tom couldn't believe his eyes. The face on the tomb looked exactly like his beloved Windy.

Windy, why is your face on this tomb ?
It's not my face Tom, it's my Mothers, replied Windy.
Your Mother was an ICE One ? Tom exclaimed. That's right Tom, but there's more. My Mother knew that it would only be a matter of time, before TRAGAS obtained her URF scan. Therefore, a successor was trained secretly.

That's right Tom.
My Mother, The ICE One
Holder of three
Has, along with her powers
Passed them to me

That's why I needed to get home, to Aylamagen, I am The ICE One, and I will lead the defense of the city. We must send word out, that anyone who has had personal contact with Hellslinger, to meet at ICE Station Eleven, along with all RAMS, and anyone with psychic training.

Nut and Bolt, I have an important mission for you. Return to Old California, as quickly as possible and inform the 'Wielders' of the situation. Though we are not allies, they may want to take advantage of this opportunity to strike from the rear.

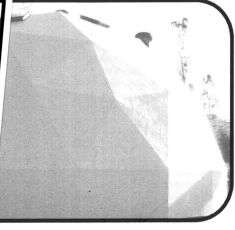

E Station Eleven

s arrive, Windy, The ICE One, waits to give instructions.

Defenders of Aylamagen, She begins. We must prevent TRAGAS from reaching the city gates, and we shall accomplish this by directing our attention to it's leader.

Killing someone provides little revenge. Even after a slow and painful death, their spirit will be released, possibly into a better place than they just departed. Only those who cared for them, if any, will continue to suffer.

But have no doubt, we could easily reach out with our amplified minds, to collapse his throat with a ghost hand, pinch off an artery to mimic a heart attack, or steer his vehicle into a fiery crash.

But I have a better plan. Together, we shall enter the mind of Lloyd E. Hellslinger 3rd.

Those of you who were brought here, because you have had personal contact with Hellslinger, will be our guides. Your memories will provide us the equivalent of a URF Scan.

A precise mixture of flashing lights and drum beats, will relax your bodies, and at the same time, stimulate your minds into overdrive.

At this point, with your permission, I shall retrieve your memories, and the imprint of Lloyd E. Hellslinger 3rd.

Once the imprint is obtained, you must leave quickly, and see that we are not disturbed, during the psychic attack. Now, let us begin.

Dancers whirl, and drummers beat, keeping pace with the flashing lights overhead. A large screen displays the likeness of the target.

As The ICE One begins, the drumming slows, and the lights go dim.

We the people of Aylamagen, beseech you, our Mother, Orbicularis, allow us to remove this threat. Open a channel, that we may protect our city, and the Bottomless Lake, from these invaders. In your name, we reach out, to protect what is ours !

Lloyd E. Hellslinger 3rd , prepare for visitors !

As the drumming and flashing lights resume, the crew find themselves slipping out of their bodies. Together they travel at incredible speed, through a lighted tunnel, while holding the target in their minds. Up ahead, they see him, Lloyd E. Hellslinger 3rd.

Night Screams

You know she's in your head
You're really gunna dread
What you know is up ahead
With those night screams
Bad dreams
Night screams

You'll be in a spiders net
Dripin pools of sweat
You really will regret
Getting those night screams
Bad dreams
Night screams

You know when they hit that switch
She'll put you in a ditch
You knew there'd be a hitch
Damn that stinking witch !
The moment you go to sleep
Your mind is hers to keep
You'll never get a wink
Without spinning down a sink

It will really make you think
You could really use a drink
Your sweat is starting to stink
You're teetering on the brink

Retreat !

Do you really want some more
Of those night screams
Bad dreams

Night screams !

Peter Pecker

Keeping chickens really is a treat.
They are the pets that are good to eat.
But leave the birds in the pen.
Each rooster with a plump hen.
Chikin Strips are here again.
Oh ! so scrumptious, with nice white meat.
Along with dumplings, they just can't be beat !
So get some money, or a welfare card
Because,
Pox E. Doodle's
Strippin Chick Chikin Strips
Are now
Sold By The Yard !
Available at all **Porkboinksters** Restaurants

Sir
Sir !
Please
Fasten
You r
Seat
Belt
And
Prepare
For
Landing

Jim doesn't know when, or if, the Colonel found out that the Cadillac was 'Hot'. There may have been a huge manhunt, if he did find out.

The Cadillac could still be alive and well in El Salvador, with the owner having no idea about how the car came to be there. Being green in color, the car could still be in use by the military.

Years later, using a self hypnosis procedure, Jim tried to recall the name of the Colonel who purchased the Cadillac. Using the information that came up, a computer search revealed an interesting story.

'Salvadoran Colonels Die In Crash'
NYTimes.com

In 1982 , Colonel Salvador Beltran Luna, Commander of an elite infantry unit, based in San Francisco Gotera, was killed along with El Salvador's Deputy Minister of Defense, when their helicopter crashed in a combat zone.

Updates to this story, if any, will be posted at;
CarThiefPriest.com

Chapter Eight
Legend of the
Singing Swords

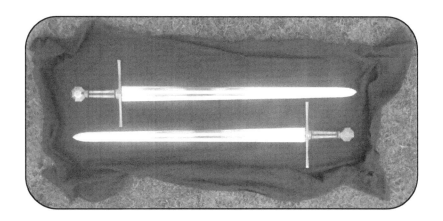

Welcome To The TH2000

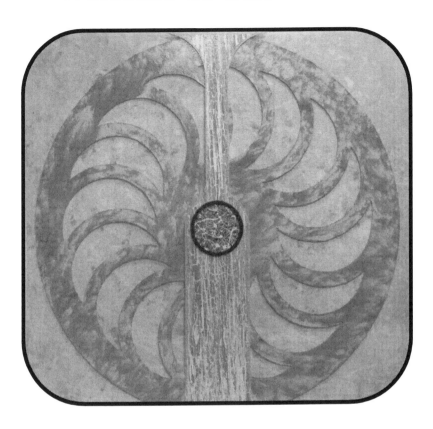

In this episode you will experience important historical events.

Just relax, as the transformation takes place.

You are on your way to an
agricultural area of old California.
At a time in the distant past.
Before the advent of
The ICE One

Transformation Complete

The White Raven

A delegation of local people have come to
The Raven for help. The symbol over his doorway
and on his chest, means that he is a
Sword for Hire.
The Wielders have many people held against their
will, being forced to work in miserable conditions
without pay.
The delegation wants Raven to kill the guards
and free the people.
Can't do it alone, he thinks to himself.
I'll have to get Hellslinger and the men.

Hellslinger Fruit Farms

South, North, West or East
Try Hellslinger's Fruits
For Your Next Feast

James L. Hellslinger

I've never been afraid to walk alone in the dark. I figure if there's something out there, it's the one that needs to be scared.

Raven, I've been waiting a long time for this day to come. Gather the men and meet me at Lewi's
I have to get Virginia, she's getting a much needed makeover.

George A. Stickman

I am not a racist, I hate all races equally.

Welcome to Lewi's Armory
I'm Lewi St. Clair, at your service.

Here she is, **Virginia** is looking good
as new and razor sharp !

Welcome to
Arch Stanton's
Arrowhead Archery
Supplies

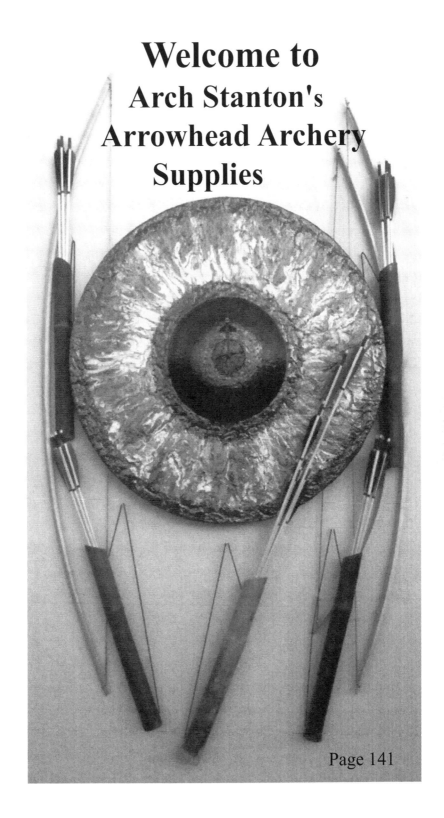

Archibald Stanton
Proprietor

Hit the Cyclops Eye
And get 10% off your purchase !

Hold Still !

On the way to the Wielder's work
camp, the men pass by a banana
plantation owned by the Wielders.
Hellslinger says to the men;
Here's a great opportunity to eliminate
some competition and get in some
cutting practice !

Crash !

Lewi gives it a try, but gets his thruster stuck in a banana tree !

Take That !

Tell me Raven, what have you learned
while studying with those psychics on
Witches Mountain, Hellslinger asked.
Raven didn't answer, but unrolled a
cloth bundle to reveal the contents.
Wow ! Exclaimed Hellslinger, those
are some beautiful swords !
Raven explained that the swords and
ancient scrolls, were found in a cave
on Witches Mountain.
Neal down my friend, asked Raven, as
he began his explanation.

Each sword is tuned differently
explained Raven. By striking the
blades to make them 'sing', and
placing one near each ear, you will
be put into a state of consciousness
that will be ideal for the battle
that lies ahead of us.

Suddenly, Hellslinger knew what must
be done.
Gather up some baskets and fruit he
ordered. Then we'll be on our way
to see **Galei Rahzin.**

Galei Rahzin
The juice from these Zee Cherries
mixed with a beverage, will put
two men to sleep for around
twenty four hours.

As Raven passes by the Wielders work camp, he yells out, **'Hellslinger fruit for sale ! Delicious Cherry Wine !**

Hey you old fool ! You can't sell Hellslinger fruit on Wielders turf.

This is what I'll do to Hellslinger !

Shish kebab, anyone ?

Delicious !

Glunk, glunk, ahhh !   Page 156

ZZZZZZZ

Out cold

Hellslinger calls to some prisoners
to open the gate.

Raven enters the open gate, goes to the
gate house
and cuts the rope, preventing the gate
from being
closed.
The imprisoned workers begin
streaming out

Nalepoc Tar

Unknown to Hellslinger and his men the work camp has a very dangerous visitor.

Nalepoc Tar, feared commander of an elite force of Mantis Warriors is on a surprise inspection of the work camp.

Kill my guards will you !

**Stand down Tar, your guards are
only sleeping.**   Page 163

I'll cut all of you to ribbons !

Let's Dance Tar !

**Down with Tar
and the Wielders**   Page 166

I'll turn you into firewood ! Page 167

Freeze Tar, I'm locked on **Tar**get !

Get ready men, I can't hold him for long.

Clank !

**Damn it ! He's nicked Virginia !
Now men, NOW !**

As Raven sneaks up and kneels down
behind Tar, Hellslinger pushes with all
his strength, and shouts **Sucker Shove !**
Get him men, and disarm him !
Get his pants !

I'll be back, with a whole legion
of Mantis Warriors !

Credits;

All songs / poems written by:
James L Parker
Including:

Khat Man Dew
Legend, In His Own Mind
Gravelsnatch !
My Crackers Are Cracked
Sean na Sagart's Tree
The ICE One Cometh
No Legged Man
Cowboy With No Hat
Escape Velocity
Night Screams

A
Production
of

Photography:
Shaun Luc Parker

RAMS
Publishing

RAMS Publishing
P.O.Box 711311
Mountain View, HI 96771 USA

Visit
CarThiefPriest.com
for any updates
on this story

Do you like big
V8 Engines ?
Check out
EngineSuperModels.com

Jim once purchased some marijuana from a new acquaintance. This is a scan of the paper that the 'weed' came wrapped in. Jim drew the circles.

el elyon Most High	enyeh I Am Becoming, I Will Be	hei na-olamim Life of All the Worlds	ha-shem The Name	m kor na-hayyim Source of Life
המקום ha-makom The Place	צור tzur Rock	שכינה shehinah Presence	מעוז חיי maoz hayai Fortress of My Life	שדי shaddai Breast / Hill, Nurturing One
אלהים elohim G*d of Creation	ריבונו של עולם ribono shel olam Master of Eternity	אין סוף ayn sof Infinite Without End	רחמנא rahamana Womb-like Compassion-ate One	אל ראי el ro-ee G*d Who Sees Me
הקדוש ברוך הוה ha-kadosh baruh hu The Holy One of Blessing	סתר לי sehter li My Hiding Place	עתיק יומין atik yomin Ancient of Days	אור מקיף or makif Surrounding Light	מעין רז ma'yan raz Well of Mystery
גלא רזין galei rah-zin Revealer of Mysteries	עזר לי ozer li My Help	אדוני adonai My Lord, Threshold, Connector	אור פנימי or p'nimi Light Within	מגן magen Shield
יוער yotzer Form Giver	תפארת tiferet Beauty	יסוד yesod Foundation	אלה ayla Power	שלום shalom Peace

Page 178